Baltimore City
Maryland

BIRTH RECORDS
1865–1894

Mary K. Meyer

HERITAGE BOOKS
2011

HERITAGE BOOKS
AN IMPRINT OF HERITAGE BOOKS, INC.

Books, CDs, and more—Worldwide

For our listing of thousands of titles see our website
at
www.HeritageBooks.com

Published 2011 by
HERITAGE BOOKS, INC.
Publishing Division
100 Railroad Ave. #104
Westminster, Maryland 21157

Copyright © 1997 Mary K. Meyer

All rights reserved. No part of this book may be reproduced or transmitted in any form or by any means, electronic or mechanical, including photocopying, recording or by any information storage and retrieval system without written permission from the author, except for the inclusion of brief quotations in a review.

International Standard Book Numbers
Paperbound: 978-1-58549-642-6
Clothbound: 978-0-7884-8799-6

INTRODUCTION

Although it is well known that the recordation of vital records in Baltimore City was required by law commencing January 1, 1875, few of us realize that prior to that date, there existed a system for keeping such records within the City. Therefore it came as somewhat of a surprise to this genealogist when this bit of information was called to her attention in 1971.

In the interest of the many genealogists with Maryland ancestors, I was privileged to borrow the original book of records in order to transcribe it for placement in the Library of the Maryland Historical Society in Baltimore. Now some 25+ years later, the idea of sharing the records with a much wider group of genealogists seems apropos. These records, dating from 1865, are not complete, i.e., they do not include every child whose birth occurred in the City of Baltimore but only for those whose parents seemed to have some interest in the exercise of recordation.

There did not seem to be any regulation or rule at just what point, i.e. age of the child, that it was required to register the birth. So we may find a great time lapse between the date of birth and the date of recordation. In some instances several years lapsed before the birth was registered and in other instances several children in a family might be registered on the very same day.

The recording of births in this particular "Register" did not come to an abrupt end in 1875 when the new law requiring recordation of births took effect. The Clerk of the Court of Common Pleas registered the birth of his own ten children on the 29th day of December 1879. The last birth recorded was dated 1904.

ABBREVIATIONS

atty.	attorney
dau.	daughter
f/b	female black
FO	father's occupation
f/w	female white
m/b	male black
m/w	male white
rec.	recorded
R.R.	Railroad

Standard abbreviations are used for names of months of the year.

- A -

Arnold, Jacob Augustus, m/w; b. 27 Aug. 1865, Baltimore, son of Conrad and Catharine Arnold. FO: Blacksmith. Rec.: 31 Aug. 1865

Adams, John Henry, m/b; b. 21 Nov. 1865; b. Baltimore, son of Benjamin and Fannie Adams. FO: Fireman St. Boat. Rec.: 30 Jan. 1866

Alexander, Charles C. m/w; b. 3 Oct. 1865, son of Charles and Julia A. Alexander. FO: Clerk. Rec: 7 May 1866

Amos, Thomas Pearson. m/w; b. Baltimore, 20 July 1866; son of Alfred P. Amos, Jr. and Elizabeth B. Amos. FO: Farmer. Rec.: 22 Jan. 1867.

Atkinson, Harry Waters, m/w; b. Baltimore, 28 March 1868; son of William George and Kate W. Atkinson. FO: Clerk. Rec.: 22 June 1868

Atkinson, Albert S., m/w; b. Baltimore, 7 Sept. 1870; son of William George and Kate W. Atkinson, FO: Clerk. Rec.: 16 Sept. 1870

Atkinson, George Wm., m/w; b. Baltimore, 16 Aug. 1872; son of William George and Kate W. Atkinson, FO: Merchant. Rec.: 30 June 1873

Atkinson, Walter Eaton, m/w; b. Baltimore, 30 Aug. 1877, son of William George and Kate W. Atkinson. FO: Merchant. Rec: 15 Feb. 1878.

- B -

Brown, James, m/w; b. Baltimore, 2 July 1865 at the Alms House; son of, unknown and Isabella Brown. FO: unknown. Rec: 10 July 1865

Baader, John Harman; m/w; b. Baltimore, 1 July 1865, son of John V. and Katharine Regina Baader; FO: Sugar Maker. Rec.: 24 July 1865

Buckey, Martha Rebecca, f/w; b. Baltimore, 8 Aug. 1865, dau of James H. and Mary Ann Buckey, FO: Engineer. Rec.: 14 Aug. 1865

Bokee, Edwin Frederick, m/w; b. Baltimore, 7 Aug. 1865, son of William H. and Mary Amelia Bokee; FO Actor. Rec.: 17 Aug. 1865

Butler, Martha Ann, f/w; b. Baltimore, 21 Aug. 1865, dau of Stephen and Sarah Butler. FO: Finisher. Rec.: 29 Aug. 1865

Blakeney, Lydia Thomas, f/w; b. Baltimore, 26 July 1865; dau. of Benjamin F. and Stella P. Blakeney, FO: Gold Pen Maker. Rec: 2 Sept. 1865

Bass, ____, m/w; b. Baltimore, 9 Sept. 1865; son of Frederick and Mary Baas. FO: Tavern Keeper. Rec.: 13 Sept. 1865

Bancroft, George Stevens, m/w; b. Baltimore, 26 Oct 1865; son of John A. and Minnie Bancroft. FO: not stated. Rec.: 4 Nov 1865

Bendann, Rose, f/w; b. Baltimore, 30 Nov. 1865; dau. of Daniel and Hannah Bendann; FO: Artist. Rec.: 14 Nov. 1865

Broadbelt, J. Eddy, m/w; b. Baltimore, 26 Sept. 1865; son of John E. and Almiri(?) Broadbelt. FO: School Teacher. Rec: 28 Dec. 1865

Beam, Josephine Ebb, f/w; b. Baltimore, 3 Aug. 1865; dau. of Joseph and Charlotte Beam. FO: Carpenter. Rec.: 29 Dec. 1865

Brown, Cassander Elizabeth, f/w; b. Baltimore, 8 Dec. 1865; dau. of George William and Sarah Ann Brown. FO: Book and Fancy store. Rec.: 2 Jan. 1866

Bell, James Robert, m/w; b. Baltimore, 26 July 1865; son of Wm. D. and Emily C. Bell; FO: Carpenter. Rec.: 2 Jan. 1866

Booz, Henrietta Maria, f/w; b. Baltimore, 30 July 1865; dau. of Edward Griffin and Matilda Booz. FO: Ship Carpenter. Rec: 4 Jan. 1866

Baker, Henry D., m/w; b. Baltimore, 12 Aug. 1865, son of James C. and Mary Ann Baker. FO: Ship Wright. Rec.: 9 Jan. 1866

Barnes, Alice, f/w; b. Baltimore, 12 July 1865, dau. of Daniel J. and Sarah J. Barnes. FO: not stated. Rec.: 11 Jan. 1866.

Brown, Mary Ann, f/w; b. Baltimore, 26 Dec. 1865, dau. of Henry C. and Mary Ann Brown. FO: Saw Manufacturer. Rec: 15 Jan. 1866

Burgess, Susannah Virginia, f/w; b. Baltimore, 10 Aug. 1865, dau. of Caleb Henry and Mary Amanda Burgess. FO: Silver Plater. Rec.: 6 Feb. 1866

Boston, C. Pinckney West, m/w; b. Baltimore, 6 Feb. 1866, son of Charles G. and Mary Cath. Boston. FO: Telegraph Operator. Rec.: 16 Feb. 1866

Byrn, Annie Vickers, f/w; b. Baltimore, 16 Sept. 1865, dau of Wm. F. and Agnes M. Byrn. FO: Sailmaker. Rec.: 21 Feb. 1865

Bradyhouse, Margaretta, f/w; b. Baltimore, 21 Sept. 1865, dau. of Thomas and Matilda Brandyhouse. FO: Boat Builder. Rec: 1 March 1866.

Boehm, Arthur, m/w; b. Baltimore, 30 Nov. 1865, son of Chas. T. and Kate S. Boehm. FO: Merchant. Rec.: 2 March 1866

Brown, Mary M., f/w; b. 19 July 1865 in Virginia, dau of John T. and Margaret A. Brown. FO: Painter. Rec.: 8 March 1866

Brentine, William Joseph, m/w, b. Baltimore, 14 July 1865, son of Aqualine and Mary Ann Brentine. FO: Trader. Rec.: 10 April 1866

Barker, Elizabeth Ann R., f/w; b. Baltimore, 18 Dec. 1865, dau. of Wm. C. and Frances Ann Barker. FO: Coal Clerk. Rec.: 24 May 1866

Bauer, Elizabeth, f/w; b. Baltimore, 26 March 1867, dau of Peter and Mary Bauer. FO: Laborer. Rec.: 28 Aug. 1867

Bauer, Rachel, f/w; b. Baltimore, 26 March 1867, dau. of Peter and Mary Bauer. FO: Laborer. Rec.: 28 May 1867

Buck, James Washington, m/w; b. Baltimore, 8 March 1867, son of John C. and Mary H. Buck. FO: Bricklayer. Rec.: 17 Sept. 1867

Broadbelt, Thomas, m/w; b. Baltimore, 8 April 1867, son of John E. and Almina V. Broadbelt. FO: Teacher. Rec.: 17 Oct. 1867

Brown, Margaretta S., f/w; b. Baltimore, 1 Aug. 1867, dau. of Stewart and Anne Brown. FO: Lawyer. Rec.: 17 Oct. 1867.

Bowman, Jacob, m/w; b. Baltimore, 14 July 1867, son of Julius and Caroline Bowman. FO: Merchant. Rec.: 4 May 1868

Boyd, Edwin Bucy, m/w; b. Baltimore, 26 Sept. 1867, son of Joseph B. and Mary L. Boyd. FO: Merchant. Rec.: 4 May 1868

Bryan, Carryl Harper, m/w; b. Baltimore, 9 March 1868, son of Wm. Shepard and Elizabeth E. Bryan. FO: Lawyer. Rec.: 23 July 1868

Bauer, George Adam Henry, m/w; b. Baltimore, 26 April 1869, son of Peter and Mary Bauer. FO: Laborer. Rec.: no date entered. See next entry.

Bauer, Frederick, m/w; b. Baltimore, 29 May 1874, dau. of Peter and Mary Bauer. FO: Laborer. Rec.: 30 May 1874

Bauer, Margaret, f/w; b. Baltimore, 29 May 1874, dau. of Peter and Mary Bauer. FO: Laborer. Rec.: 30 May 1874

Barnet y Ruiz, Carlos, m/w; b. Baltimore, 22 Dec. 1869 son of Joaquin and Amalia Ruiz y Barnet. FO: Analytical Chemist. Rec.: 20 Oct. 1879

Bowersock, Albeert Curtis, m/w; b. Baltimore, 8 Dec. 1874, son of A. and Emma Bowersock. FO: Not stated. Rec.: 11 June 1937. (N.B: Papers in document file in vault, Bureau of Vital Statistics.]

- C -

Constance, Virginia Lee, f/w; b. Baltimore, 3 July 1865, dau of John George and Ida Constance. FO: Shoemaker. Rec.: 27 Dec. 1865

Cruse Joseph H., m/w; b. Baltimore, 1 Nov 1865, son of Joseph A. and Annie R. Cruse. FO: Machinist. Rec: 9 Jan. 1866.

Collins, Georgianna Boyce, f/w; b. Baltimore, 23 July 1865, dau of George W. and Anne Rebecca Collins. FO: Clerk. Rec.: 28 Feb. 1866

Crowley, Adoniram Judson, m/w; b. Baltimore, 9 Jan. 1866, son of Wm. S. and Eleanor H. Crowley. FO: Blacksmith. Rec.: 24 June 1866.

Clark, Isabella Catharine, f/w: b. Baltimore, 17 Sept. 1865, dau. of Thos. S. J. and Harriet C. Clark. FO: Clerk. Rec.: 7 March 1866.

Chandler, Archibald Louis, m/w; b. Baltimore, 27 July, 1866, son of D. F. and Harriet C. Clark. FO: None. Rec.: 3 Jan. 1867

Cooper, William H., m/w; b. Baltimore, 17 Dec. 1867, son of Sam'l. and Elizabeth A. Cooper. FO: Machinist. Rec. 22 July 1877.

Crowle, Mary Virginia, f/w; b. Baltimore, 28 July 1867, dau. of John A. and Carrie Virginia Crowle. FO: Liquor Dealer. Rec.: 18 Jan. 1868.

Chandler, Alice Maud, f/w; b. Baltimore, 10 Dec. 1868, dau. of Dan'l and Sarah Louisa Chandler. FO: None. Rec. 3 July 1868

Clark, Mary Agnes, f/w; b. Baltimore, 10 July 1870, dau. of Augustus B. and Mary M. CLark. FO: Conductor. Rec.: 23 June 1871

Claypoole, Robert Garland, m/w; b. Baltimore, 31 March 1875, son of James Y. and Mollie H. Claypoole. FO: Clerk. Rec.: 3 April 1875.

Claypoole, James Yeardsley, Jr., m/w; b. Baltimore, 4 June 1876; son of James Y. and Mollie H. Claypoole. FO: Clerk. Rec.: 12 Sept. 1876.

Claypoole, Genevieva, f/w; b. Baltimore, 10 Nov. 1879, dau. of James Y. and Mollie H. CLaypoole. FO: Clerk. Rec.: 9 Dec. 1879

Claypoole, Martha Ann, f/w; b. Baltimore Co., 13 Oct. 1881, dau. of James Y. and Mollie H. Claypoole. FO: Clerk. Rec.: 15 Oct. 1881.

Claypoole, Edward Brown, m/w; b. Baltimore City, 20 Dec. 1883, son of James Y. and Mollie Claypoole. FO: Clerk. Rec.: 24 Dec. 1883.

- D -

Dryden, Henry Hartman, m/w; b. Baltimore, 6 July 1865, son of James and Mary Ellen Dryden. FO: Blacksmith, Rec: 8 July 1865

Drill, Sallie B., f/w; b. Baltimore, 13 July 1865, dau. of James M. and Sallie T. Drill. FO: Agent, N.C.R.R. Rec: 21 July 1865.

Dutton, Donaldson Lowry, m/w; b. Baltimore, 9 Aug. 1865, son of Frederick W. and Louisa A. Dutton. FO: Clerk. Rec.: 17 Aug. 1865.

Duffer, William, m/w; b. Baltimore, 12 Sept. 1865, son of George J. and Hannah Duffur [sic]. FO: Wire Worker. Rec.: 13 Oct. 1865.

Debaufre, Thomas Edward, m/w; b. 24 July 1865, Baltimore, son of Wm. H. and Sarah A. Debaufre. FO: Shoe Store. Rec.: 30 Oct. 1865

Dalrymple, John Howard, m/w; b. Baltimore, 24 July 1865, son of Wm. D. and Emily I. Dalrymple. FO: Physician. Rec: 1 Nov. 1865.

Daiger, Robert E. Lee, m/w; b. 9 Aug. 1865, Baltimore, son of M. A. and Pamelia A. Daiger. FO: Cabinet Maker. Rec.: 27 Nov. 1865.

D_____. b. 10 July 1865, Baltimore. No further information.

Deutch, Joseph, m/w; b. 10 July 1865, Baltimore, son of Dr. Solomon and Augusta Deutsch. FO: Clergyman. Rec.: 2 Jan. 1866.

Dutton, Mary Florence, f/w; b. Baltimore, 9 Sept. 1865, dau of John R. and Annie M. Dutton. FO: Clerk. Rec. 8 Feb. 1866.

Dennis, Mabel, f/w: b. Baltimore, 1 Jan. 1866, dau. of William H. and Lydia A. Dennis. FO: Bricklayer. Rec.: 21 Feb. 1866.

Dobson, William James, m/w; b. Baltimore, 9 Oct. 1865, son of James T. and Ellen A. Dobson. FO: Painter. Rec.: 12 March 1866.

Danneker, Henry Winter Davis, m/w; b. Baltimore, 16 Oct. 1865, son of David H. and Elizabeth G. Daneker. FO: Custom House Official. Rec: 27 March 1866.

Dual, Isaac Alexander, m/w; b. Baltimore, 26 Oct. 1865, son of William Chapman and Eliza Jane Deal; FO: Plumber. Rec.: 12 April 1866.

Delevie, Eliah I., m/w; b. Baltimore 23 Aug. 1865, son of Isaac I. and Betsey I. Delevie. FO: Merchant. Rec: 14 May 1866

Dixon, Ida May, f/w; b. Baltimore, 29 May 1866, dau. of Bradley S. and Jane E. Dixon. FO: Merchant. Rec.: 19 June 1866.

Dickinson, Frank Newton, m/w; b. Baltimore, 19 Sept. 1866; son of James A. and Elizabeth A., Dickinson. FO: Book Keeper. Rec.: 9 Nov. 1866.

Dillow, Ellen V., f/w; b. 29 Jan. 1867, Baltimore, son of Jno. R. and Martha E. Dillow. FO: Tinner. Rec.: 10 May 1867

DeBaufre, Sarah Ann, f/w; b. Baltimore, 27 Jan. 1867; dau. of Wm. and Sarah Ann DeBaufre. FO: Shoe Business. Rec. 24 June 1867.

Dutton, William Burneston, f/w; b. Baltimore, 8 May 1867, son of Frederick W. and Louisa A. Dutton. FO: none given. Rec: date not shown.

Dempsey, Charles Barry, m/w; b. Baltimore, 17 March 1868, son of John B. and Louisa J. Dempsey. FO: Book Keeper. Rec.: 5 May 1868

Dorsey, William Thomas, m/w; b. Baltimore, 11 Nov. 1867, son of William Thos. and Ann Noble Dorsey. FO: Farmer. Rec.: 17 July 1868.

Dillow, John R., m/w; b. Baltimore, 4 Feb. 1868, son of John R. and Martha E. Dillow. FO: Tinner. Rec.: 19 July 1868

Daffin, Francis Dawes, m/w; b. Baltimore, 11 Jan. 1868; son of F. D. and Mary Ida Daffin. FO: Printer. Rec: 17 Aug. 1869.

Daffin, Mary Emma, f/w; b. Baltimore, 11 May 1869, dau. of F. D. and Mary Ida. FO: Printer. Rec.: 17 Aug. 1869.

Dempsey, CLara Lee, f/w; b. Baltimore, 3 Oct. 1871, dau. of John B. and Louisa J. Dempsey. FO: Bookkeeper. Rec.: 26 Feb. 1872.

DeBernardy, Henry Sarphine Gustav Vicomte, m/w; b. Baltimore, 6 Oct. 1873, son of Henry Vicomte and Gustina DeBernardy. FO: None. Rec.: 8 Dec. 1873.

Dempsey, John Butler, Jr., m/w; b. Baltimore, 20 April 1874, son of John B. and Louisa J. Dempsey. FO: Bookkeeper. Rec.: 3 Sept. 1874.

- E -

Elliott, Walter Foxhall, m/w; b. 18 July 1865, Baltimore, son of Edward and Margaret Ann Elliott. FO: Notion Business. Rec: 24 July 1865.

Emmons, Howard Mann, m/w; b. 15 Nov. 1865, Baltimore, son of Herman L., Emmons, Jr. and Jennie Lathrop. FO: None given. Rec.: 2 May 1866.

- F -

Fulton, Mabel, f/w; b. Baltimore, 4 July 1865, dau. of Albert K. and Laura Fulton. FO: Printer. Rec.: 11 July 1865.

France, John A., m/w; b. Baltimore, 21 Sept. 1865, son of Peter and Catharine France. FO: Tailor. Rec.: 10 Oct. 1865.

Finkeldey, Henry Julius, m/w; b. Baltimore, 13 Oct. 1865, son of Henry J. and Catharine Finkeldey. FO: Currier. Rec.: 20 Oct. 1865.

Falcimagne, Marie Bertha, f/w; b. Baltimore, 3 Dec. 1865, dau. of Frederick M. and Celeste M. Falcimagne. FO: Apothecary. Rec: 6 Jan. 1866.

Fisher, Florence Addelia, f/w; b. Baltimore, 11 Feb. 1866, dau. of William H. and Ann Addelia Fisher. FO: Cigar Manufacturer. Rec: 20 Feb. 1866.

Fogle, Ida Estelle, f/w; b. Baltimore, 17 Feb. 1866; dau. of John H. and Sarah F. Fogle. FO: Clerk. Rec.: 16 July 1866.

Friedman, Theresa, f/w; b. Baltimore, 10 Dec. 1865, dau. of Seml[?] and Mary Friedman. FO: Clothier. Rec.: 21 Feb. 1866.

Friedman, Isaac, m/w; b. Baltimore, 23 Feb. 1867, son of Seml[?] and Mary Friedman. FO: Clothier. Rec.: 8 Mar. 1867.

- G -

Gade, Emeline, f/b; b. at the Alms House, Baltimore, 5 July 1865; father unknown, mother: Jane Jade [sic]. MO: unknown. Rec.: 10 July 1865

Gill, Roger Taney, m/w; b. 15 July 1865, Baltimore, son of N. Rufus and E. Agnes D. Gill. FO: Atty-at-Law. Rec.: 30 Sept. 1865.

Goldsborough, Charles Lawrence, m/w; b. Baltimore 4 Oct. 1865; son of Jno. Thomas and Caroline Va. Goldsborough. FO: Engineer. Rec.: 2 Nov. 1865

Geddes, Alexander, m/w; b. Baltimore, 3 Nov. 1865, son of James W. and Sarah Ann Geddes. FO: Tinman, Rec: 6 Nov. 1865.

Goghegan, Arthur Holliday, m/w; b. Baltimore, 23 July 1865, son of Philemon and Margaret A. Goghegan. FO: Shipwright. Rec.: 19 Jan 1866.

Gentry, Alfred St. John, m/w; b. Baltimore, 5 Oct. 1865, son of Haden and Annie A. Gentry. FO: Telegraph Operator. Rec.: 4 April 1866.

Gesine, Eleanore, f/w; b. Baltimore, 4 July 1866, dau. of Christopher and Ellen M. H. Gesine. FO: Merchant. Rec: 24 July 1866.

Gebhart, John Morris, m/w; b. Baltimore 25 Oct. 1865, son of William and Caroline S. Gebhart. FO: Wheelwright. Rec: 24 Oct. 1866.

Goldman, Benjamin, m/w; b. Baltimore, 13 Nov. 1866, son of Lewis, Jr. and Anna Goldman. FO: Clothier. Rec.: 8 March 1867.

Graham, William W., m/w; b. Baltimore, 13 Jan. 1867, son of James R. and Annie R. Graham. FO: Jeweler. Rec. 13 April 1867.

Gill, Julia Rebecca, f/w; b. Baltimore, 28 March 1867, dau. of N. Rufus and E. Agnes D. Gill. FO: Atty-at-Law. Rec.: 27 April 1867

Goldman, M., m/w; b. Baltimore, 21 April 1867, son of S. and Hester Goldman. FO: Storekeeper. Rec.: 10 May 1867.

Gelbach, William H., m/w; b. Baltimore, 5 Feb. 1868, son of Wm. H. and Lotta Gelbach. FO: Broker. Rec.: 20 Aug. 1868.

Girvin, Florence L., f/w; b. Baltimore, 21 Feb. 1868, dau. of Jas. A. and Charlotte E. Girvin. FO: Clerk. Rec.: 21 Aug. 1868.

Gill, Rufus Dowson, m/w; b. Baltimore, 1 Feb. 1869, son of N. Rufus and E. Agnes D. Gill. FO: Atty-at-Law. Rec.: 29 June 1869.

Gutermuth, Albert V., m/w; b. Baltimore, 28 July 1869, son of Valentine and Julia A. Gutermuth. FO: Tailor. Rec.: 20 Jan. 1870.

Gill, Robert Lee, m/w; b. Baltimore, 20 De.c 1870, son of N. Rufus and E. Agnes D. Gill. FO: Atty-at-Law. Rec.: 23 Feb. 1871.

Gutermuth, Emma Matilda, f/w; b. Baltimore, 15 July 1875, dau. of Valentine and Julia Gutermuth, FO: Tailor. Rec.: 14 Feb. 1872.

Gill, Robert Sydney, m/w; b. Baltimore, 11 March 1875, son of N. Rufus and E. Agnes D.. FO: Atty-at-Law. Rec: 8 Dec. 1875.

Gill, Nicholas Howard, m/w; b. Baltimore, 14 Nov 1876, son of N. Rufus and E. Agnes D. Gill. FO: Atty-at-Law. Rec. : 25 May 1877.

Gill, Anna Agnes, f/w; b. Baltimore, 7 Sept. 1879, dau. of N. Rufus and E. Agnes D. Gill. FO: Atty-at-Law. Rec.: 29 Oct. 1879.

Gill, Henry May, m/w; b. Baltimore, 9 Nov. 1861, son of N. Rufus and E. Agnes D. Gill. FO: Atty-at-Law. Rec.: 29 Sept. 1880.

Gill, Edward George, m/w; b. Baltimore, 25 Jan. 1863, son of N. Rufus and E. Agnes D. Gill. FO: Atty-at-Law. Rec.: 29 Sept. 1880.

Gill, Calvert Burke, m/w; b. Baltimore, 3 Feb. 1883, son of N. Rufus and E. Agnes D. Gill. FO: Atty-at-Law. Rec.: 24 April 1884.

- H -

Hildebrand, Lewis Henry, m/w; b. Baltimore, 6 July 1865, son of Henry and Margaretha Hildebrand. FO: Barber. Rec.: 13 July 1865

Heckrotte, Henry William m/w; b. Baltimore, 25 July 1865, son of Henry William and Margaret V. Heckrotte. FO: Tobacconist. Rec: 1 Aug 1865,

Hobday, Alma Elizabeth, f/w; b. Baltimore, 25 July 1865, dau. of Edward and Elizabeth Jane Hobday. FO: Property Broker. Rec.: 9 Aug. 1865.

Hollstein, Lavinia, f/w; b. Baltimore, 7 Aug. 1865, dau. of John C. and Mary Emma Hollstein. FO: Merchant. Rec.: 11 Sept. 1865.

Haupt, Marietta, f/w; b. Baltimore, dau. of Charles M. and Elizabeth B. Haupt. FO: Tobacconist. Rec.: 23 Oct. 1865.

Harmoe, John Henry, m/w; b. Baltimore, 25 Sept. 1865, son of John Henry and Ann Harmoe. FO: Restuarant. Rec.: 25 Oct. 1865.

Hilberg, Francis, m/w; b. Baltimore, 20 Nov. 1865, son of John A. and Nettie V. Hilberg. FO: Clerk. Rec.: 15 Dec. 1865

Henderson, Landonia, f/w; b. Baltimore 28 Aug. 1865, dau. of Sam'l S. and Josephine Henderson, FO: Shoemaker, Rec. 26 Dec. 1865.

Horwitz, Samuel Gross, m/w; b. Baltimore, 5 Oct. 1865, son of Benjamin F. and Louisa Gross Horwitz. FO: Lawyer. Rec: 3 Jan. 1866.

Hengst, Annie Leah, f/w; b. Baltimore, 4 July 1865, dau. of Benjamin and Mary Hengst. FO: Minister. Rec.: 10 Jan. 1866.

Harrison, Annie, f/w; b. Baltimore 13 July 1865, dau. of N. S. and Elizabeth Harrison. FO: Lightening Rod Dealer. Rec.: 13 Jan. 1866.

Hohn, Caroline, f/w; b. Baltimore, 30 July 1865, dau. of Francis and Josephine Hohn. FO: Sugar Maker. Rec.: 17 Jan. 1866.

Heath, William George, m/w; b. Baltimore, 13 Dec. 1865, son of Elisha S. and Harriet S. Heath. FO: Merchant. Rec.: 31 Jan. 1866.

Henderson, Louisa Lincoln, f/w; b. Baltimore, 12 July 1865, dau of James and Louisa Henderson. FO: Machinist. Rec.: 31 Jan. 1866.

Hartmann, Philip John, m/w; b. Baltimore, 12 Oct. 1865 son of Hermann B. and Mary E. Hartmann. FO: Tailor. Rec.: 3 Feb. 1866.

Hess, Adelaide Louisa, f/w; b. Baltimore, 19 Jan. 1866, dau. of Isaac, Jr. and Mary Hess. FO: Clerk. Rec.: 14 May 1866.

Hanson, Ida Elizabeth, f/w; b. Baltimore, 4 Jan. 1866, son of Wm. H. and Cath. R. Hanson. FO: Harness Maker. Rec.: 7 June 1866

Hissey, Mary Ann, f/w; b. Baltimore, 9 Dec. 1865, dau of John A. and Caroline Hissey. FO: Carter. Rec.: 8 June 1866.

Hess, George Wm., m/w; b. Baltimore, 23 Aug. 1866, son of George H. and Agnes C. Hess. FO: Machinist. Rec.: 5 Sept. 1866.

Henderson, Margaret Josephine, f/w; b. Baltimore, 17 Jan. 1867, dau of Sam'l and Josephine Henderson. FO: Shoemaker. Rec.: 5 March 1867.

Harmoe, Anna M. A., f/w; b. Baltimore, 10 Jan. 1867, dau. of John Henry and Anne Harmoe. FO: Machinist. Rec.: 26 April 1867.

Hartman, Mary Catharine, f/w; b. Baltimore, 7 May 1867, dau. of George F. and Ellen M. Hartman. FO: Clothier. Rec.: 24 May 1867.

Hobday, Erastus Lord Edward, m/w; b. Baltimore, 12 Sept. 1867, son of Edward and Elizabeth Jane Hobday. FO: Broker. Rec: 21 Sept. 1867.

Hobday, Alma Elizabeth, f/w; b. Baltimore, 12 Sept. 1867, dau. of Edward and Elizabeth Jane Hobday. FO: Broker. Rec.: 21 Sept. 1867.

Hollstein, Bernard, m/w; b. in Baltimore, 6 Jan. 1868, son of John C. and Mary Emma Hollstein. FO: Merchant. Rec.: 16 July 1868.

Haupt, Ella Virginia, f/w; b. Baltimore, 20 Feb. 1868, dau. of Chas. M. and Lizzie A. Haupt. FO: Cigar Maker. Rec.: 20 Aug. 1868

Hartsell, Cornelia Virginia, f/w; b. Baltimore, 19 July 1868, dau of John W. and Amanda M. A. P. Hartsell. FO: Milk Driver. Rec: 12 Jan. 1869.

Hook, Charles Howard, m/w; b. Baltimore, 3 Jan. 1874, son of Jacob W. and M. Anna Hook. FO: Clerk. Rec.: 20 Oct. 1876.

Hoffman, Ellen, f/w; b. Baltimore, 3 Nov. 1878, dau. of J. L. and Olivia F. Hoffman. FO: Salesman. Rec.: 15 April 1879.

- I -

No individuals with names starting with I were recorded.

- J -

Jentner, Anna M., f/w; b. Baltimore, 5 Sept. 1865, dau. of Geroge and Caroline Jentner. FO: not stated. Rec.: 5 March 1866.

Jordan, Mary E., f/w; b. Baltimore, 22 July 1864, dau. of Thomas J. and Mary Jane Jordan. FO: Plasterer. Rec.: 8 March 1866.

Joyce, Franklin Pierce, m/w; b. Baltimore, 26 April 1867, son of John and Airey Ann Joyce. FO: Carpenter. Rec.: 7 Oct. 1867.

Johns, Edith, f/w; b. Baltimore, 19 Jan. 1868, dau. of Henry V. D. and Annie Eliza Johns. FO: Manufacturer. Rec.: 29 July 1868.

- K -

Kellett, William George, m/w; b. Baltimore, 17 July 1865, son of Benjamin and Mahaley Kellett. FO: Grinder. Rec. 24 Aug. 1865

Kuhling, John Adam, m/w; b. Baltimore, 5 Aug 1865, son of George Theodore and Regina Kuhling. FO: Tavern Keeper. Rec.: 31 Aug. 1865.

Kahl, Augusta Bertha Amelia Christina, b. Baltimore, 8 July 1865, dau. of Charles Wm. Albert and Catharine Annie Kuhl. FO: Pocket Book Maker. Rec: 18 Sept. 1865.

Kelly, Elizabeth Dorry, f/w; b. Baltimore, 11 Sept. 1865, dau. of Henry W. and Fanny Smith Kelly. FO: Tobacconist. Rec.: 28 Sept. 1865

Knoebel, Henry Washington, m/w; b. Baltimore,.9 Oct. 1865, son of Henry and Ann Knoebel. FO: Liquor Dealer. Rec: 24 Oct. 1865.

Kirk, Fanny Augusta, f/w; b. Baltimore, 7 Jan. 1866, dau. of R. Edwin and Sidney A. Kirk. FO: Lock Manufacturer. Rec.: 6 Feb. 1866.

Kepler, Samuel C., m/w; b. Baltimore, 20 July 1868, son of Adolph and Charlot Kepler. FO: Physician. Rec.: 3 Aug. 1868.

Keller, Elizabeth Davis, f/w; b. Baltimore, 9 Sept. 1868, dau. of Peter E. and Catherine Keller. FO: Milk Driver. Rec.: 12 Jan. 1869.

- L -

Lowry, Charles Lefaivre, m/w; b. Baltimore, 8 Oct. 1865, son of William P. and Maggie M. Lowry. FO: Clerk. Rec.: 14 Nov. 1865.

Linthicum, Ellen, f/w; b. Baltimore, 24 July 1865, son of Thaler (?) A. and Emma S. Linthicum. FO: Lawyer. Rec.: 3 Jan. 1866.

Leech, William Henry, m/w; b. Baltimore, 22 April 1865, son of David and Annie Leech. FO: Bar Keeper. Rec: 3 Feb. 1866.

Lamb, Arthur Lincoln, m/w; b. Baltimore, 2 Sept. 1865, son of Eli M. and Anna W. Lamb. FO: Teacher. Rec.: 2 March 1866.

Lewis, George Edward, m/w; b. Baltimore, 11 Aug. 1866, son of George F. and Julia Ann Lewis. FO: Reporter. Rec.: 14 Aug. 1866.

Lemmon, Jos. C., m/w; b. Baltimore, 24 Nov. 1865, son of Jos. F. and June (Jane?) E. Lemmon. FO: Printer. Rec.: 21 Sept. 1866. (NB: the initial "B" is written over the word "Jos.")

Lefevre, Kate, f/w; b. Baltimore, 7 July 1866, dau. of J. A. and Kate L. Lefevre. FO: Minister of G. Rec.: 14 March 1867.

Lowry, Walter Benson, m/w; b. Baltimore, 12 Feb. 1867, son of Wm. P. and Maggie M. Lowry. FO: Clerk. Rec.: 7 May 1867

Little, Henry Benjamin, (the letters "enjam" are crossed out in the original", m/w; b. Baltimore, 26 Nov. 1866, son of Thomas A. and Sarah Jane Little. FO: Clerk. Rec.: 24 May 1867.

Lowenbach, Alfred, m/w; b. Baltimore, 24 May 1868, son of Moritz and Bertha Lowenbach. FO: Merchant. Rec.: 23 Nov. 1868.

Lefevre, George, m/w; b. Baltimore, 16 Sept. 1869, son of J. A. and Kate L. Lefevre. FO: Clergyman. Rec.: 2 Dec. 1869.

Lowenbach, Camill, f/w; b. Baltimore, 12 Dec. 1869, dau. of M. and Bertha Lowenbach. FO: Merchant. Rec.: 9 Sept. 1870.

- M -

Miller, John Marshall, m/w; b. Baltimore, 3 July 1865, son of Jacob P., Jr. (of NY) and Irene L.(?) Miller. FO: Clerk. Rec.: 7 July 1865.

Myers, Rosa, f/w; b. Baltimore, 8 July 1865, dau. of Lewis and Sarah Meyers. FO: Drover. Rec.: 19 July 1865.

Maynard, Edgar Phillips, m/w; b. Baltimore, 14 July 1865, son of Geoge W. and Josephine C. Maynard. FO: Mill Wright. Rec.: 24 July 1865.

Miller, George Philip, m/w; b. Baltimore, 30 Jan. 1865, son of George W. and Charlotte Miller. FO: Segar Maker. Rec.: 5 Aug. 1865

McCarthy, ____, f/w; b. Baltimore, 14 July 1865, dau. of Patrick and Mary McCarthy. FO: Huckster. Rec.: 10 Aug. 1865.

Miller, James E., m/w; b. Baltimore, 7 Aug. 1865, son of Joseph and Sarah Ellen Miller. FO: Iron Moulder. Rec.: 16 Aug. 1865.

Mann, Mary B., f/w; b. Baltimore 27 Aug. 1865, dau. of George W. and Hannah Mann, FO: Soldier. Rec.: 1 Sept. 1865.

McCahan, Edward Emory, m/w; b. Baltimore, 24 Oct. 1865, son of Ed. Luther and Elizabeth Ann McCahan. FO: Clerk. Rec.: 2 Nov. 1865.

McGuire, Evalyn L., f/w; b. Baltimore, 7 July 1865, dau of Thomas C. and Matilda A. McGuire. FO: Clerk. Rec.: 14 Nov. 1865.

McCreary, Charles D., m/w; b. Baltimore, 1 July 1865, son of Jno. W. and Sarah E. McCreary. FO: Printer. Rec.: 30 Dec. 1865.

McGill, George Washington, m/w; b. Baltimore, 24 Nov. 1865, son of Thos. J. and Anne E. McGill. FO: Caulker. Rec: 2 Jan. 1866.

Mathews, John Oliver Bazil, m/w; b. Baltimore, 6 June 1865, son of William J. and Elizabeth Mathews. FO: Gas Fitter. Rec.: 4 Jan. 1866

Moore Ella, f/w; b. Baltimore, 28 Feb 1866, dau. of Cicero A. and Eleanor Miller. FO: Merchant. Rec.: 2 April 1866.

McGough, Edward Alexander, m/w; b. Baltimore, 11 April 1866, son of Patrick and Sarah McGough. FO: Florist. Rec.: 13 April 1866.

Moses, Carrie, f/w; b. Baltimore, 4 Dec 1865, dau. of W. B. and Henrietta Moses. FO: Tobacconist. Rec.: 7 May 1866.

Medinger, Elizabeth Pfaff, f/w; b. Baltimore, 9 Feb. 1866, dau. of Augustus C. and Hannah R. Medinger. FO: Merchant. Rec.: 26 July 1866.

Murray, Alice Lilly, f/w; b. Baltimore, 29 Dec. 1865, dau. of O. B. and Alice Murray. FO: Broker. Rec.: 24 Dec. 1866.

Moore, Robert James, m/w; b. Baltimore, 26 March 1866, son of Geo. W. and Annie Moore. FO: Constable. Rec.: 6 April 1867.

Moore, Eleanora, f/w; b. Baltimore, 19 July 1867, dau. of Cicero A. and Eleanor Moore. FO: Merchant. Rec.: 30 Aug. 1867.

McNeir, Wm. Stewart, m/w; b. Baltimore, 16 Aug. 1867, son of Wm. J. and Laura J. McNier. FO: Clerk, Rec.: 30 Aug. 1867.

Madden, Ada May, f/w; b. Baltimore, 29 Aug, 1867, dau of James and Emily J. Madden. FO: Plumber. Rec.: 25 Oct. 1867.

Medinger, A. Christoph, m/w; b. Baltimore, 8 Jan. 1868, dau. of Augusta [sic] C. and H. P. Medinger. FO: Merchant. Rec.: 2 July 1868.

Medinger, John Leib, m/w; b. Baltimore, 4 March 1868, son of John G. and M. Medinger. FO: Merchant. Rec.: 20 July 1868.

McNeir, Alice Genevieve, f/w; b. Baltimore, 12 Sept. 1869, dau. of Wm. J. and Laura J. McNeir, FO: Clerk. Rec.: 3 Aug. 1871.

Medinger, Henrietta R., f/w; b. Baltimore, 12 April 1877, dau. of Augustus C. and Hannah R. Medinger. FO: Merchant. Rec.: 25 May 1877.

- N -

Nixdorf, Annie E., f/w; b. Baltimore, 22 Aug 1865, dau. of Tobias S. and Susan Nixdorff. FO: Clerk. Rec.: 14 Nov. 1865.

Norwood, Frank h., mw; b. Baltimore, 12 Oct. 1865, son of Belt S. and Isabella Norwood. FO: Carpenter. Rec.: 5 April 1866.

Nolen, Carrie Wallace, f/w; b. Baltimore, 12 Oct 1865, dau. of Louis and Elizabeth V. Nolen. FO: U. S. Army. Rec.: 7 May 1867.

Norwood, Robert Jackson, m/w; b. Baltimore, 25 June 1867, son of Belt S. and Isabella Norwood. FO: Carpenter. Rec.: 6 Dec. 1867.

Nierman, Charles Edward, b. Baltimore, 14 July 1868. No further information recorded.

- O -

O'Brien, John C., m/w; b. Baltimore, 3 Jan. 1865, son of Wm. J. and Kate O'Brien, FO: Lawyer. Rec.: 4 Nov. 1865.

Orem, Beall Sherman, m/w; b. Baltimore, 8 July 1865, son of J.[?] Baily and Carrie P. Orem. FO: Officer, U. S. A. Rec.: 14 Dec. 1865.

Opitz, Chas. Wm., m/w; b. Baltimore, 27 Dec. 1865, son of John and Elizabeth M. Opitz. FO: Segar Maker. Rec.: 10 Feb 1866.

Orem, Kisziah M., f/w; b. Baltimore, 5 June 1865, dau. of William G and ____ Orem. FO: Stone Cutter. Rec.: 8 June 1866

- P -

Pollack, Flora, f/w; b. Baltimore 5 Sept. 1865, dau of Uriah A. and Helen Pollack. FO: Merchant. Rec. 13 Feb. 1866.

Pollack, Jeanette, f/w; b. Baltimore, 5 Jan. 1865, dau. of Uriah A. and Helen Pollack. FO: Merchant. Rec.: 13 Feb. 1866.

Pilson, Millard Anderson, m/w; b. Baltimore, 9 Feb 1866, son of John T., Jr. and Emily Pilson. FO: Painter. Rec.: 10 March 1866.

Perine, William Redgrave, m/w; b. Baltimore, 9 Jan. 1866, son of Wm. H. and Emily E. Perine. FO: Constable. Rec.: 4 Oct. 1866.

Poe, Margaretta, f/w; b. Baltimore, 7 July 1866, dau. of John Prentiss and Anna J. Poe. FO: Lawyer. Rec. 6 Nov. 1866.

No children with names starting with Q were recorded.

- R -

Reinhart, Geo. Henry Edward, m/w; b. Baltimore, 10 July 1865, son of George P. and Mary A. S. Rinehart. FO: Clerk. Rec. 18 Oct. 1865.

Register, Edward Church, m/w, b. Baltimore Co., son of Sam'l Wilson and Clara Register. FO: Clerk. Rec.: 2 Jan. 1866.

Ridgaway, George Thomas, m/w, b. Baltimore, 30 July 1865, son of Thomas S. and Georgianna Ridgaway. FO: Clerk. Rec.: 6 Jan. 1866.

Rainer, Charles E. B., m/w; b. Baltimore 24 Nov. 1866, son of Joseph A. and Martha V. Rainer. FO: Tinner. Rec.: 14 May 1866.

Rayman, Annie Mary Florence, f/w; b. Baltimore, 4 May 1866, dau. of Albert B. and Elizabeth Rayman. FO: unknown. Rec. 2 Aug. 1866.

Reinhart, Charles Schaefer, m/w; b. Baltimore, 9 July 1866, son of George P. and Mary A. E. Reinhart. FO: Unknown. Rec.: 18 Dec. 1866.

Rosenstein, Clara, f/w; b. Baltimore, 3 Dec 1866, dau. of Simon and Marcelline M. L. Rosenstein. FO: Clerk. Rec.: 15 March 1867.

Randolph, Barthelomew, m/w; b. Baltimore, 2 Jan. 1867, son of James T. and Mary G. Randolph. FO: Insurance Officer. Rec.: 25 April 1867.

Reinhart, Albert Reginald, m/w; b. Baltimore, 31 March 1868, son of George P. and Mary A. E. Reinhart. FO: Clerk. Rec.: 15 July 1868

Reinhart, Percy Lee, m/w, b. Baltimore, 25 Feb. 1871, son of George P. and Mary Reinhart. [The letters "Madg" appear to be written over the word "Mary" and a second name, Jane is added.) FO: Clerk. Rec.: 20 Oct 1871.

Rasin, Martha Annie, f/w; b. Baltimore, 8 March 1863, dau. of Isaac Freeman and Julia Ann Rasin. FO: Clerk of the Court of Common Pleas. Rec.: 29 Dec. 1879.

The following children of the above couple, all b. in Baltimore, were recorded the same date as above:

Genevieve Ringold Rasin, b. 17 April 1865

Howard Claypoole Rasin, b. 24 July 1866

John Freeman Rasin, b. 28 Oct. 1869

Morris Claypoole Rasin, b. 11 Feb. 1872

Gertrude Brown Rasin, b. 22 __ 1876

Julia Angela Rasin, b. 18 Sept . 1877

Helen Ringold Rasin, b. 17 Aug. 1879

Carroll Wilson Rasin, b. 4 June 1881

Alice Regina Rasin, b. 5 July 1883

- S -

Skeahan, _____, m/w; b. Baltimore, 18 July 1865, son of Thomas and Mary Skeahan. FO: Laborer. Rec.: 10 Aug. 1865.

Strong, Laura E., f/w; b. Baltimore, 24 July 1865, dau. of James E. and Margaret Strong. FO: Varnisher. Rec.: 1 Sept. 1865.

Strong, Louisa Jane, f/w; b. Baltimore, 24 July 1865, dau. of James E. and Margaret Strong. FO: Varnisher. Rec: 1 Sept. 1865

Stellmann, Louise, f/w; b. Baltimore, 3 Sept. 1865, dau. of John and Sarah Ann Stellmann. FO: Merchant. Rec. ___ 1865.

Sheckells, Harry Clifton, m/w; b. Baltimore, 26 Sept. 1865, son of John and Sarah Ann Sheckells. FO: Clerk. Rec.: 11 Oct. 1865.

Smith, George Ferdinand, m/w; b. Baltimore, 3 July 1865, son of Ferdinand Chas. and Annie Catharine Smith. FO: Cabinet Maker. Rec.: 14 Oct. 1865.

Smith, Augusta Adell, f/w; b. Baltimore 2 June 1865, dau. of Joseph S. and Lavinia C. Smith. FO: Grocer. Rec.: 28 Oct 1865.

Somerville, Ida May, f/w; b. Baltimore, 14 Oct 1865, dau of Harrison and Elizabeth J. Somerville. FO: Gardener. Rec.: 25 Nov. 1865.

Speed, William George, m/w; b. Baltimore, 20 Nov. 1865, son of Christopher C. and Mary E. Speed. FO: Clerk. Rec.: 2 Dec 1865.

Spencer, David Williamson, m/w; b. Baltimore, 9 July 1865, son of Jarvis and Julianna J. Spencer. FO: Atty-at-Law. Rec.: 6 Jan. 1866.

Shaffer, Caroline Christopher, f/w, b. Baltimore, 9 Feb. 1866, dau. of Charles H. and Catharine J. Shaffer. FO: Caster (Carter?). Rec.: 5 March 1866.

Squires, Mary M., f/w; b. Baltimore, 18 Sept. 1865, dau of John O. and Mary E. Squires. FO: Carpenter. Rec.: 8 March 1866.

_____. b. Virginia, 19 July 1865. No other information stated.

Stockett, Christianna Williams, f/w; b. Baltimore, 29 Dec. 1865, dau. of Charles H. and Anna M. Stockett. FO: Painter. Rec.: 14 March 1866.

Sheldon, Margaret, f/w; b. Baltimore, 25 Sept. 1865, dau. of John and Elizabeth Sheldon. FO: Shoemaker. Rec.: 19 March 1866.

Shamer, Martha E., f/w; b. Baltimore, 25 Sept. 1865, dau. of Theodore and Mary J. Shamer. FO: Chair Maker. Rec.: 20 March 1866.

Stewart, Mary Elizabeth, f/w; b. Baltimore, 24 March 1866, dau. of James and Sarah Elizabeth Stewart. FO: Tailor. Rec.: 3 April 1866.

Starr, George, m/w; b. Baltimore, 14 Nov. 1865, son of William T. and Elizabeth D. Starr. FO: Tinner. Rec.: 14 May 1866.

Street, George W., Jr. m/w; b. Baltimore, 3 April 1866, son of George W. Sr. and May Jane Street. FO: Clerk. Rec.: 12 June 1866.

Smith, Harry Dewitt, m/w; b. Baltimore, 17 June 1864, son of Edgar D. and Mary C. Smith. FO: Clerk. Rec.: 20 July 1866

Slattery, Elizabeth A., f/w; b. Baltimore, 22 Nov. 1865, dau. of Wm. Hayes and Catharine E. Slattery. FO: Barber. Rec.: 4 Oct. 1866.

Sweglar, Robert E. Lee, m/w; b. Baltimore, 25 Aug. 1866, son of Jos. R. Sweglar. FO: Machinist. Rec. 8 Oct. 1866.

Stempel, Maria Elizabeth, f/w; b. Baltimore, 23 Sept. 1866, dau. of Julius and Victoria M. Stemple. FO: not stated. Rec.: 19 Jan. 1867.

Schirm, Louisa, f/w; b. Baltimore, 18 Dec 1866, dau. of Conrad and Antonetta Schirm. FO: Tailor. Rec.: 10 May 1867

Slattery, Thomas Francis, m/w; b. Baltimore, 9 Aug. 1867, son of Wm. H. and Catharine E. Slattery. FO: Chairmaker. Rec.: 11 Dec 1869

Swinney, Willis, m/w; b. Baltimore, 22 Aug. 1869, son of Epaphroditus and Elizabeth P. Swinney. FO: Lawyer. Rec.: 1 June 1868 [sic].

Shryock, Henry Soliday, Jr., [sic], b. Baltimore, 15 Oct. 1881, son of Richard Fuller and Maggie B. Shryock. FO: Lawyer. Rec.: 1 Dec. 1881.

The following children of the above couple were recorded as follows:

George Forney Shryock, b. Baltimore, 5 April 1883; Rec.: 12 Oct 1883

Richard Fuller Shryock, Jr., b. Baltimore, 8 Sept. 1884; Rec.: 20 Nov. 1884

Shryock, Fannie Marie Hoeltzcke, b. Baltimore 26 Sept. 1885; Rec.: 2 Dec. 1885

Shryock, John Carter, b. Baltimore, 28 Jan. 1889. Rec.: 10 July 1889

- T -

Tuttle, ____, m/w; b. Baltimore, 15 July 1865, son of Michael and Honora Tuttle. FO: Labourer. Rec.: 10 Aug. 1865.

Thiede, Emma Louise, f/w; b. Baltimore, 3 July 1865, dau. of William F. and E. Pietsch Theide. FO: Watch Maker. rec.: 20 Dec. 1865.

Taylor, Grafton P., m/w; b. Baltimore, 16 Sept. 1865; son of Joseph L (S?) and Annie B. Taylor. FO: Clerk. Rec: 12 Jan. 1866.

Thomson, Wm. Baltzar, m/w; b. Baltimore, 2 Dec. 1865, son of John D. and Eliza Tomson. FO: Clerk. Rec.: 14 May 1866.

Tilghman, Harriet, f/w; b. Baltimore, 4 Sept. 1866, dau. of, James and Sarah A. Tilghman. FO: Mariner. Rec.: 20 Sept. 1866.

Teepe, Emma Louisa, f/w; b. Baltimore, 4 Sept. 1866, dau. of Henry and Louisa Teepe. FO: Merchant. Rec.: 10 Oct. 1866.

- U -

No individuals with names starting with U were recorded.

- V -

VanReuth, Edward Chester Felix Marie, m/w; b. Baltimore, 7 April 1867, son of Edward Charles Felix and Mary Ann VanReuth. FO: Artist. Rec.: 27 May 1867.

Vincente, Edward Howard, m/w; b. Baltimore, 9 Nov 1869 son of Edward P. and Margaret Vinzente [sic]. FO: Coach Maker. Rec.: 21 Nov. 1869.

Vincente, Elsie Marcelino, f/w; b. Baltimore, 25 Sept. 1878, dau. of E. P. and Margaret Vincente. FO: Coach Maker. Rec.: 29 Sept. 1878.

Vansant, Joshua Hunell, m/w; b. Baltimore, 7 Sept. 1878, son of James W. and Ida Ophelia Vansant. FO: Clerk. Rec.: 6 April 1904.

Vansant, Hiram Duryea, m/w; b. Baltimore, 2 April 1880, son of James W. and Ida Ophelia Vansant. FO: Clerk. Rec.: 6 April 1904.

Vansant, James Menzies, m/w; b. Baltimore, 21 April 1894, son of James W. and Ida Ophelia Vansant. FO: Clerk. Rec.: 6 April 1904.

- W -

Work, Sarah E., f/w; b. Baltimore 12 Sept. 1865, dau. of William L. and Mary E. Work. FO: Ship Joiner. Rec.: 2 Jan. 1866.

Wilson, Amy, f/w; b. Baltimore 3 Dec. 1865, dau. of James M. and Amy S. Wilson. FO: Minister. Rec.: 2 Jan. 1866.

Williams, Rosa Lee, f/w; b. Baltimore, 17 Oct 1865, dau of Dr. James Thomas and Juliet Duke Williams. FO: Physician. Rec.: 8 Jan. 1866.

Waller, Carr, m/w; b. Baltimore 2 Nov. 1865, son of Dr. Wm. N. and Annie Mary W. Waller. FO: Physician. Rec.: 8 Jan. 1866.

Wilkens, Frederick Henry, m/w; b. Baltimore, 8 Nov. 1866, son of Henry and Theresa Wilkens. FO: Merchant. Rec. 9 April 1866.

Wheatley, Ambrose, m/w; b. Baltimore, 8 Oct. 1865, son of John and Charlotte Ann Wheatley. FO: Tailor. Rec.: 9 April 1866.

Welsh, Lucy Carroll, f/w; b. Baltimore, 19 Feb. 1866, dau of Charles E. and Eliza C. Welsh. FO: Tobacco Mer. Rec.: 14 April 1866.

Wroth, Margaret Elizabeth, f/w; b. Baltimore, 29 April 1866, dau. of Dr. Wm. J. and Louisa A. Wroth. FO: Doctor of M. Rec.: 15 Oct 1866.

Whittle, Harry Boone, m/w; b. Baltimore, 29 Dec. 1866, son of C. N. and Maggie S. Boone, FO: Clerk. Rec.: 7 May 1867.

Wiegel, Adelaide Blanche H., f/w; b. Baltimore, 30 April 1867, dau. of Wm. Henry and Elizabeth Ann Wiegel. FO: U. S. Army. Rec.: 7 June 1867.

Warnick, Virginia Lee, f/w; b. Baltimore, 23 Aug 1867, dau. of John F. and Mary Ann Warnick. FO: Clerk. Rec.: 10 Feb. 1868.

Wilson, Henry John, m/w; b. Baltimore 17 Feb. 1868, son of H. Wm. and Mary J. Wilson. FO: Drayman. Rec.: 16 May 1868.

Welsh, William, m/w; b. Baltimore, 13 Sept 1867, son of John and Josephine Welsh. FO: not stated. Rec.: 14 July 1868.

Wiegel, Willie Gilmore, Jr., m/w; b. Baltimore, 6 June 1869, son of Wm. Henry and Elizabeth Ann Wiegel. FO: Not stated. 13 Oct. 1869.

Wild, Chas. Fred'k. Nicholas. m/w; b. Baltimore, 25 Aug. 1869, son of John F. and Regina Wild. FO: Whip Maker. Rec.: 3 Jan. 1870.

Warnick, Edwin Booth, m/w; b. Baltimore, 24 Nov. 1872, son of John F. and Mary A. Warnick. FO: Whip Maker. Rec.: 11 June 1873

- X, Y, Z -

No individuals with names starting with X, Y or Z were recorded.

Other Heritage Books by Mary K. Meyer:

A Directory of Cayuga County Residents Who Supported Publication of the History of Cayuga County, New York

Abstracts from Madison County, New York Newspapers in the Cazenovia Public Library

Baltimore City Birth Records, 1865–1894

Cemetery Inscriptions of Madison County, New York, Volume 1
Mary K. Meyer and Joyce C. Scott

Deaths, Births, Marriages from Newspapers Published in Hamilton, Madison County, New York, 1818–1886
Mrs. E. P. Smith, Joyce C. Scott and Mary K. Meyer

Divorces and Names Changed in Maryland by Act of the Legislature, 1634–1867

Free Blacks in Harford, Somerset and Talbot Counties, Maryland 1832

Meyer's Directory of Genealogical Societies in the U.S.A. and Canada: 1998–2000, 12th Edition
Family of Mary K. Meyer

Westward of Fort Cumberland: Military Lots Set Off for Maryland's Revolutionary Soldiers

Who's Who in Genealogy and Heraldry 1990
Mary K. Meyer and P. William Filby